Make Your Own
Weather Station

Terry Jennings

OXFORD
UNIVERSITY PRESS

OXFORD
UNIVERSITY PRESS

Great Clarendon Street, Oxford OX2 6DP

Oxford University Press is a department of the University of Oxford.
It furthers the University's objective of excellence in research, scholarship,
and education by publishing worldwide in

Oxford New York

Athens Auckland Bangkok Bogotá Buenos Aires Calcutta
Cape Town Chennai Dar es Salaam Delhi Florence Hong Kong Istanbul
Karachi Kuala Lumpur Madrid Melbourne Mexico City Mumbai
Nairobi Paris São Paulo Singapore Taipei Tokyo Toronto Warsaw

with associated companies in Berlin Ibadan

Oxford is a registered trade mark of Oxford University Press
in the UK and in certain other countries

Published in the United Kingdom
by Oxford University Press

Text © Terry Jennings 2000

The moral rights of the author have been asserted

Database right Oxford University Press (maker)

First published 2000

British Library Cataloguing in Publication Data

Data available

ISBN 0 19 915708 1

Available in packs
Weather Pack of Six   (one of each book)   ISBN 0 19 915711 1
Weather Class Pack   (six of each book)   ISBN 0 19 915712 X

Printed in Hong Kong

Acknowledgements

The Publisher would like to thank the following for permission
to reproduce photographs:

British Broadcasting Corporation: p 4; Corel: p 10; Robert Harding Picture
Library/Christopher Nicholson: p 20; Frank Lane Picture Agency/Brian
Cosgrove: p 11, 16; Frank Lane Picture Agency/D. Warren: p 19 (*bottom
left*); Frank Lane Picture Agency/Bruce Henry: p 19 (*right*); Mark Mason:
Cover and title page; Science Photo Library/Hank Morgan: p 5.

Illustrations by Julian Baker, Andy Cooke, and Martin Salisbury.

Contents

Weather forecasts

You can see weather forecasts on television and in newspapers. A weather forecast suggests what the weather is going to be like. Weather forecasts can help you decide what to do for the day, and what clothes to wear.

Weather forecasters tell us what they think the weather is going to be like.

Weather stations

The people who make weather forecasts work in a weather station. They collect facts about the weather. Weather forecasters measure how hot or cold it is. They measure how windy it is and how much rain falls.

A scientist watching the weather at the Meteorological Office.

You can make your own weather station. This book will show you how.

Hot or cold?

Sometimes when we are outside we feel hot, sometimes we are cold. Some clothes keep us warm, others keep us cool. On a windy day we can feel very cold.

Heat from the sun

Whether we feel hot or cold depends mainly on the heat from the sun. The hottest days are in summer when the sun shines and there are no clouds. This is because the sun heats the earth which then warms the air around us.

Temperature and thermometers

Temperature is a measure of how hot or cold
it is. We measure temperature with a thermometer.
A thermometer shows how hot or cold the air is.
It shows the temperature in degrees. Each mark
on the thermometer is one degree Celsius. We write
it as 1°C.

It is a
hot day. ▶

It is a very cold
day. Water
freezes at this
temperature. ▶

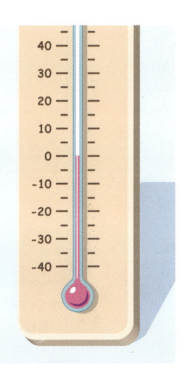

Make your own thermometer

Make your own thermometer to see how hot or cold it is.

You will need

plastic bottle with a screw cap

plastic drinking straw

scissors

sticky tape

thick card

modelling clay

coloured water

What to do

1 Ask an adult to drill a hole in the bottle cap.

2 Fill the bottle with water.

3 Put the cap on the bottle and push a drinking straw through the hole. Pack modelling clay around the straw. ▼

4 Fix a strip of card behind the straw. Leave the water to settle, then mark the water level on the card. ▼

5 Stand the thermometer in a bowl of cold water. See the water level in the straw fall. ▶

6 Ask an adult to put the thermometer in a bowl of warm water. See the water level in the straw rise.

7 Stand the thermometer on a shelf. See how the water level changes as the air temperature changes.

 Clouds

The heat of the sun makes all our weather. The sun shines every day, but we cannot always see it if there are clouds in the sky. Clouds block out some of the sun's light and heat.

The main kinds of cloud

Clouds come in all shapes and sizes but there are three main kinds.

cirrus clouds

cumulus clouds

stratus clouds

The three main kinds of cloud are cirrus, cumulus, and stratus

Cirrus clouds are thin wisps of cloud, high in the sky. They often show that warmer weather is coming.

Cumulus clouds look like giant tufts of cotton wool. We see them on warm, sunny days. When cumulus clouds grow tall and dark, there may be rain or a thunderstorm.

Stratus clouds are low and grey. They form a blanket across the sky. Stratus clouds bring drizzle, or snow if it is very cold.

Thunderstorms come from the biggest cumulus clouds. They are tall and dark and have a flat top.

Make a cloud frame

A cloud frame makes it easier to draw the clouds you see.

You will need

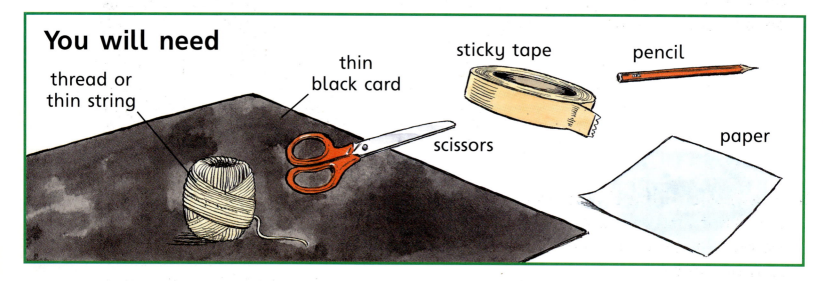

thread or
thin string

thin
black card

sticky tape

pencil

scissors

paper

What to do

1 Ask an adult to help you cut the thin black card into two "L" shapes.

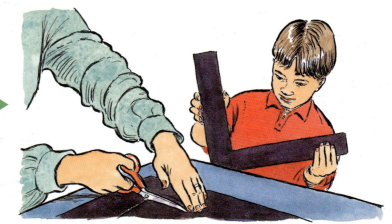

2 Tape the two pieces of card on a window and watch the clouds passing by.

3 Draw some of the clouds you see. What kind of weather do we have when you see each kind of cloud?

4 Tape two pieces of thread or thin string across the middle of the cloud frame.

5 How much of the cloud frame is covered by clouds? Is it a quarter, a half, three-quarters, or is it all of the cloud frame?

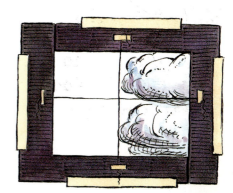

Rain and snow

Rain makes puddles of water on the ground. The puddles soon dry up, but the water does not go away. It turns into an invisible gas called **water vapour**. The water vapour rises into the air.

Making clouds

The sun turns water to vapour all the time. When the vapour cools high in the sky it turns into millions of tiny drops of water. These make clouds.

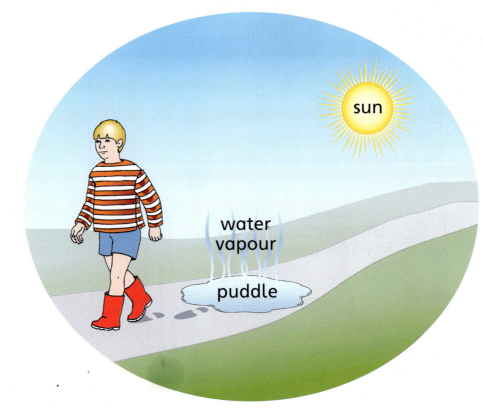

sun

water vapour

puddle

Falling rain and snow

When the drops of water bump into each other they make bigger drops, which fall to the ground as rain. If it is very cold, the water droplets in the clouds may freeze and turn into small pieces of ice. These fall to the ground as snow.

All our rain comes from clouds. Water never goes away. It is in the sea, lakes, and rivers, in the air as **water vapour**, or as water droplets in the clouds, or in the soil.

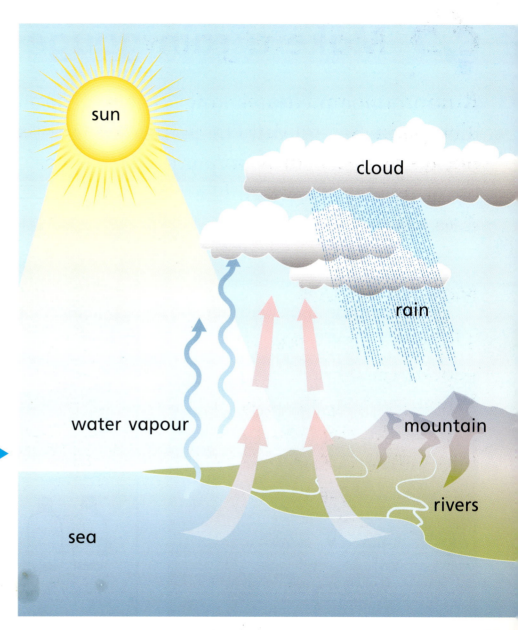

sun

cloud

rain

water vapour

mountain

rivers

sea

Make a rain gauge

A rain gauge measures how much rain has fallen. The picture below shows a real rain gauge but it is quite easy to make a rain gauge of your own.

A rain gauge that weather forecasters use.

You will need

labels

scissors

sticky tape

large plastic bottle

box of sand

pen

7 small bottles the same size

What to do

1 Ask an adult to cut the top off the bottle. ▼

2 Put the top back on the bottle upside down. Fasten it with sticky tape.

3 Take the rain gauge outside. Stand it in a box of sand to stop it from blowing over. ▼

4 Look at your rain gauge every morning. Put each day's rain into a small bottle. Label the bottle with the day of the week. When did most rain fall? On which days did no rain fall?

 # Wind

Wind is moving air. We cannot see the wind, but we can feel it and hear it.

Why winds blow

Winds blow because the sun warms some parts of the earth more than others. The warmer parts of the earth warm the air above them. The warm air rises. Cold air rushes in to take its place. As the air rushes in, it makes a wind.

How winds form ▶

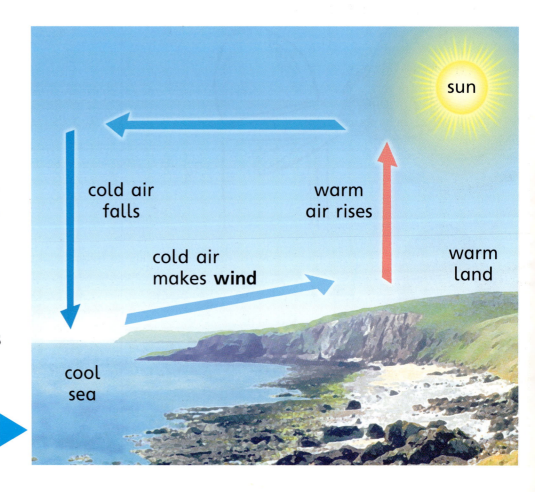

sun

cold air
falls

warm
air rises

cold air
makes **wind**

warm
land

cool
sea

Breezes and gales

Wind brings different weather – hot or cold, wet or dry. When the wind blows only slightly, we call it a breeze.

On a breezy day, a kite flies well.

A gale is a very strong wind. Gales can damage buildings and uproot trees.

How hard is the wind blowing?

This is an anemometer. It measures how hard the wind is blowing. The harder the wind blows the faster the little cups turn.

You will need

paper plate

drawing pin

4 paper cups

stick

brush

paints

sticky tape

What to do

1 Tape four paper cups round the plate. Paint one cup a bright colour so you can see it when it turns round.

2 Ask an adult to help you fasten the paper plate on top of the stick with a drawing pin. Make sure that the plate turns easily. ▼

3 Take your anemometer outside. See how fast it turns in the windiest place around your school.

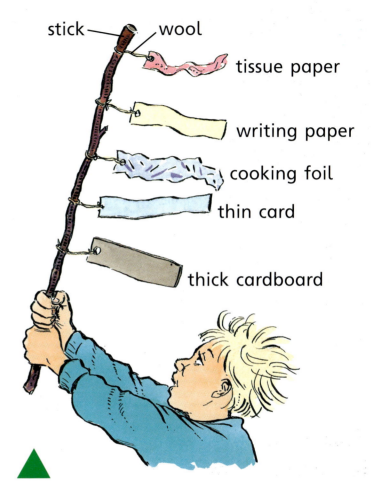

stick — wool

tissue paper

writing paper

cooking foil

thin card

thick cardboard

▲

This is another way of seeing how hard the wind is blowing. The harder the wind blows, the more flags are lifted up.

 # Make a weather chart

Weather forecasters collect facts about the weather. They collect the facts on a chart. Then they say what they think the weather is going to be like.

Forecast the weather

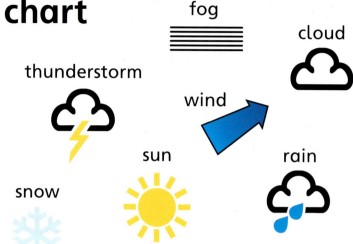

fog

cloud

thunderstorm

wind

sun

rain

snow

Copy this weather chart on to a piece of paper.
Say what you think the weather is going to be like tomorrow.
Use the weather signs above.

Tomorrow is...	I think the weather will be...	The weather was...
Tuesday		
Wednesday		
Thursday		
Friday		
Saturday		
Sunday		
Monday		

Recording the weather

On the next day, go outside and see what the weather is really like. See what your weather **instruments** are doing. Then put the right weather signs and information in your weather chart.

Was your forecast as good as the one on the television or radio? Fill in your chart each day.

Glossary

freezes Gets so cold that it becomes hard.

instruments Tools that help in work, usually for measuring.

water vapour Water has been warmed so that it turns into a gas.

Index